Between Me and All Harm

Ann Zell

for Mairead

— Ann Zell

23 Feb - 05

SUMMER PALACE PRESS

First published in 2005 by

Summer Palace Press
Cladnageeragh, Kilbeg, Kilcar, County Donegal, Ireland

Printed by Nicholson & Bass Ltd.

A catalogue record for this book is available
from the British Library

ISBN 0 9552122 0 0

This book is printed on elemental chlorine-free paper

for Drue

Acknowledgments

Some of the poems in this book have appeared in: *The Black Mountain Review; HU; The SHOp; Windows;* and in *Art Words: an Ulster anthology of visual and verbal art* (Coleraine, Cranagh Press 2001); *You Can't Eat Flags for Breakfast* (New Belfast Community Arts Initiative 2001).

I would like to thank the Tyrone Guthrie Centre, Annaghmakerrig, for the time and space to work on this collection, and Belfast City Council for an Arts Bursary.

Biographical Notes

Ann Zell was raised in a large family on a small farm in Idaho.

After university she worked in an aircraft factory in California, and lived for some years in New York where she worked for a small publisher. She moved to London, and after twenty years, to Ireland.

She has worked as a secretary, researcher, printer and typesetter. Before starting to write seriously in the mid 1980s, she spent most of her energy in various radical campaigns.

Her first collection, *Weathering*, was published by Salmon Press in 1998.

She is settled in West Belfast, and goes each year to the beach in Cloughglass townland, in the Rosses of Donegal, which is the location for many of these poems.

She is a member of the Word of Mouth Poetry Collective and her work has been included in *The Word of Mouth Anthology* (Blackstaff Press, 1995); *The White Page* (Salmon, 2000); and the *Field Day Anthology Vol. V* (CUP 2003).

CONTENTS

Slow train
for Robin and Barbara

Every night, at the end of our field
on a parallel with Carcassone

the transcontinental express went by
and left me with a yen to travel

reinforced at the age of twelve
returning home from hospital

in a carriage full of khaki soldiers
going on leave before Japan.

Living now where light diminishes
like the last breath of someone dying

at peace with herself, I forget how fast
dark falls at lower latitudes

obscuring the wagons of the army train
draped in the colour of my regret

the vernissage of tiled roofs
on show from my hotel balcony.

Is Barbara still painting sunrise
from the terrace of the bergerie

if wind and weather let her?
Oh, the South of France, friends sighed

envisaging the opposite
of our reluctant Belfast spring

as I set off to visit kin
I hadn't seen for twenty years.

Finding by luck the both of you
confounds my family of fears.

When my grandmother got the vote

She might have been a suffragette,
but had many children and no transport.

On election day, she took her place
behind the horses, beside her husband
driving into town.

Halfway there
he asked her how she meant to vote,
and turned the wagon round.

Swan watch in the Bog Meadows

Sunday morning –
St Galls and St Louise's shut
and St James still asleep

I could almost be back
in the bird-rich field between the highway and the slough
where I coached my brothers for their merit badges

and where we took Delwyn Barrett, four years old,
to watch him spot the make and model
of every car that passed, from its outline.

He grew up to be an ornithologist.
I can't tell one small bird from another
these days, they flit so fast.

In the pond beside the motorway
a new-hatched shopping trolley
gleams among the rushes

and there's one brown super-egg
untended on the swan's nest.
The nest looks shambolic, a mistake.

Fearing the worst,
mindful of last year's stoning,
I have no eyes for flotillas of lesser birds.

Monday morning –
birdsong against a drone of cars.
No egg, no swans. Instead

two Canada geese occupy the nest
standing as tall as they can
aloof from a clatter of goslings.

I'm composing a letter to the paper, lamenting
the cruelty of the youth, when the swans
sail in from nowhere with four grey cygnets.

The cob chases the squatters across the pond.
The pen and her babies climb on board.
Feeling daft, feeling happy, I cycle home.

Cycle song

A musical child with airs to spare
I took no heed when my grandmother warned
that whistling girls and crowing hens
would always come to some bad end.

Whistling kept me good company
on the long desert roads where I cycled through
feelings that rose and fell like the staves
of the telegraph wires and their metal hum.

And whistling got me past the dog
that lay in wait on the way to school
although my nonchalant descant
was counterpoint to grounded fear.

These days I cycle in Donegal
where the dogs sleep at the side of the road
with one eye open. I haven't the breath
to whistle, and you wouldn't know what they'd do.

Grotte de Niaux

Shadows
bobbing in the light of our hand lamps

we follow the guide up the dry bed
of the river that carved this catacomb,
to the Salon Noir
   where the lights are turned off
and we experience dark.

I think I know what this cave holds, but
when the guide's torch flares
I am unprepared

for the familiar ibex bison horses deer
who come wide-eyed out of the rock
        across millennia
to meet our silence and our stares.

Unprepared for the rush of tears.

Someone will come

Mondays, soak tub wash tub rinse tub
the gathered smell of bleach and sunlight
Tuesdays, sprinkle and press

I take the washing off the racks and put it where it goes.
Trousers sweaters towels in the airing cupboard
T-shirts turtlenecks socks bras knicks
in their various drawers in the skip-salvaged bureau
sheets straight back on the bed.

My ironing skills perfected on the shirts of seven brothers
are never exercised.

Necklaces hang from the mirror posts
the ring my daughter made crowns the featureless
head of my bronze serpentine muse
bracelets adorn the Przewalski horse picked up for ten pence
at close of trade in Cheshire Street
between fighting the fascists and Sunday brunch
down Brick Lane.

the Sunday my mother ambushed me
at age thirteen, with white lace gloves for church;
a patent leather purse

Front room furniture
sits politely, rehearsing conversations.
Books I've saved to read again
when I can't remember whodunnit,
the loot from years of beachcombing,
anticipatory toys.

The tuning light on the kitchen radio
glows red when I get close. TV works best
with living flesh as the antenna.

Jobs as simple as chopping onions pose the question
Why? Who cares if I still make white sauce
the exact way my mother taught me; stews that end up
frozen, to flavour ends of the month?

I savour solitude, but I cannot cook small portions.

I cannot crack a breakfast egg
without remembering

the giver of the eggcup,
my grandfather's toast soldiers
and how we thought his eating habits very English

the stirring excitement of oatmeal mush
– Yellowstone Park in a pan –

the world widened by my father's assertion
that some people, somewhere
ate it with salt and butter.

Receive and transmit.

Within a matrix of repeated actions
the space between one swallow and another
the hollows of the day
they come.

Arrival

for Lauren

A bird I'd never seen before
stopped on the branch outside my window
while I was making a praise-poem

about how you landed among us
as the last day dawned
resembling no one but yourself.

Between one word and another
it was gone, feathers spilling silver
from the risen winter sun.

You are too new for praising.
I hold you and the bird and silver
in the same curved thought.

First sighting

Twilight on the deserted beach.
Some grey animal too big for a cat with no look of a dog

moved down from the rocks and across the foreshore
loping, stopping, leaping through last year's bent grass
and the seaweed left by winter storms.

From the chalet window
I imagined a minuscule deer, because of
its long back, its bounding, high hindquarters,
and what could have been a pair of horns

until it came close
and sat up facing me with its ears twitching
and I realised, *Hare.*

A second hare followed,
sniffing the trail of the first as if it couldn't see
those erect signalling ears through the long grass,
or maybe because it liked the smell,
and they jinked off into the legend of this place
flashing white scuts like giant powder puffs.

Two mundane relatives of theirs
repeated the run the next night
but by then my mind was on other things –

oyster catchers gliding across the wet sand on no visible legs,
that morning's perfect double rainbow,
walking at low tide to an island brilliant with larks –

and I thought this poem was finished
and rightly titled.

So long from home I'd forgotten
the rabbits with jackass ears we shot at for fun,
with .22's and BB guns.

Time, like a ticking crocodile

My big brother and I
who will both grow up
to interrogate old bones

play under the magic
circle of the kitchen table
believing ourselves invisible.

Around us my mother moves
busy with Christmas baking.
Unseen suits her.

Already in love with dinosaurs
and their descendants
he can't wait

to give me my present
and I can't wait to open it.
We take turns

evading the snatch of its jaws
the switch of its tail
its clockwork slow advance.

Christmas morning
my mother is wearing
her told-you-so face

and there it is
dead on my chair
but I don't care.

My brother is a sober man
focused on eternity.
I've learned a different lesson.

Time has swallowed
half my friends.
Open your presents early.

Twelfth Morning, Falls Park

Tearaways on mountain bikes
yodel down the river path.
Twins ascend the hill

resplendent
in a double buggy
with a fringe on top.

The river is low
and full of junk, but
it gurgles satisfactorily

past a primitive forest
of horsetail ferns, rhododendrons
stealing a march,

feathery trees
the ivy's claimed
for climbing frames.

Helicopters
have all gone south
for the day. I sit

on the stump of a tree
that outlived its civic function
thinking

poetry will not
save us. Writing it
anyway.

Sandstream

Where the tide went out along the cliff
it left a narrow stretch of sand
scattered with cuttlebones of squid
like tiny styrofoam bodyboards.

Sand you could walk on, sit in, lie on, imprint.
Lauren sifted it through a plastic riddle,
Emily and Kay made channels,
tunnels to entice the sea.

I sat and watched our outlines soften
gradually, as grains of sand
fell into the gravity well.
Returned to Belfast still obsessed with sand.

When you rang from London about New York
I had no comfort. Wanted to tell you
crying was a human response
and better than my frozen silence

but sand was blowing through my head,
figures falling from a tower,
horror at those innocent deaths,
the retributive deaths to come.

Recycling

Biking this dedicated level path against the flow
of motorway traffic hellbent for Fast City

I jettison the doctrine of no pain no gain for a new
belief in minimum effort, maximum reward.

Past docks and ferry ports, the turpentine high
of the lumber yards, the reek from meat processing plants

the self-drive, self-storage, self-help
portacabins and sheds of bootstrap commerce

the tree-screened landfill site where gulls
swoop on fresh garbage, it hits you –

a great fragrant weedy billow of purple and yellow
wildflowers and broom: the lough opening out in possibility.

Block out the roar of the cars and hear the slurp of small waves
coming ashore in the wake of the high-speed ferry.

Birds and men dig in the tidal mud. Adrift from perceived
allegiances, people who resemble me are taking their leisure.

Collect shells. Reclaim sea-turned glass the shade of green
I'm looking for. Reject somebody's T-shirt, chest size 34.

Tunnel vision

First thing this morning
a blackbird pulled an elastic earthworm
out of the ground and down its gullet
just like that.

Next thing this morning
the sun rose at six and again at seven
as the clock went forward,
leaving me

stuck in that swallowed hour
with the worm translating into food,
the blackbird doing its high-wire act
on the power line.

Notes of an amateur naturalist

Cloughglass Strand, Donegal, February 2003

I

Hard-packed sand, the tide far out.
White gulls against a ground of blue
unmarked by contrails. A break

shadowed by the news that south of here
while I'm studying the habits
of residents and winter visitors

birds of passage from my home place
are touching down at Shannon
to refuel en route for the Gulf.

II

The other mammal on the beach
– a man my age with local knowledge –
heads for the intertidal zone

and I follow, asking questions, taking note.
He points to what looks like black plastic
melted onto a rock, and starts to pick.

Tells me what it is and how you cook it.
I chew a handful, copying. Spit it out.
Genus *Porphyra.* Laver, nori, sleabhac.

III

Ignorant of the life cycles of gastropods,
I can't explain the dearth (apart from
limpets, whelks and periwinkles)

of species my guide to the Irish seashore
claims should be flourishing here.
Blame it on the cold. Fallaciously

attribute to less complex fauna
my human reaction to horror:
hide, if you can, until it's over.

Given

Misreading the clock
I set day in motion too early

to do anything but drink coffee,
mourn lost mornings in Donegal

and watch, from the upstairs window
overlooking the street

a yellow-and-grey
Water Board worker on a bike

the Royal nightshift coming home
in colour-coded fatigues

an old man
fighting his black umbrella

two backpackers
on the trail of their spreadout map

and opposite, on one roof
in a ridge of grey roofs

colonised by moss and lichen
(*why that roof in particular?*)

a colloquy
of pigeons descended from rock doves

stretching Modigliani necks
against a bone-china sky.

A tongue that curls

Her mother holds her up
and they communicate in tongues
profile to profile

flicking a ping pong
ball of love
back and forth between them.

The first time I saw her
I recognized her tongue,
out taking the air

tasting its environment.
A tongue like that shows
talent and heredity.

Now she lies on my couch
in Belfast, a winter visitor
eight weeks old

deciphering the twisting codes
that tell her: woman, human,
her tongue doing all the work.

You probably don't remember me
for Agnes

As if I could ever forget the girl who played with me
when I had eczema. I remember your don't-care laugh

the long red hair my mother found dangerous,
the freedom of your house.

Still living in Jefferson County beside the river
you wrote after all this time, and I meant to answer . . .

I'm glad to hear you've got ten grandchildren
and hay is selling well this year.

My life in foreign parts has not been that exciting.
Do you remember how we spent every recess

pumping up on the swings, standing face to face
exchanging breath, straining and lifting

and showing our pants to the boys
as we tried to go over the bar?

Rainbow

Promises! Nevertheless
after the forecaster's delight of a changeable day
the last downpour ends.

Clouds keep their distance
and behind them the rays of a low sun
bestow what I once thought of as heaven's glory
on the long hill of Aranmore.

Something flutters silver on a point of rock.
Thrashing like a paddle steamer, a magpie
lifts – somehow – and somehow flies.
Then, ailerons up, landing gear out,
glides down to perch, *voila*, with a flourish of fans.

The wind has dropped. Late-to-migrate swifts
and the window-frame spiders hanging out in their webs
are looking for dinner, while the midges dine on me.

Listening to Fauré on the classics channel
instead of the lecture on how to combat global warming.
Thinking – like a deity with schadenfreude – *apres moi le deluge.*

Older than I want to be.

March is a lion
for Susie

What the gale couldn't lift or shift
or drill a way through, it tried to flatten.
Moonwalking over spongy turf
wild grass and resting heather

storm glutting my senses
and my thoughts on staying upright,
I saw no cars on the road,
boats at sea, beasts in the field

no other wind-struck walkers, until
I met a woman with tangled hair
who spread out her arms
and yelled, *Isn't it wonderful!*

illuminating the day like sheet lightning.

Convergence

She comes through the airport checkpoint
with the baby in a sling, the other two kids
in moonstruck orbit around her. Meeting

always surprises me, as if she's the piece
of the jigsaw you swear is lost, turned up
by accident to begin to finish the puzzle

and I'm never sure what she means until
it's time for her to leave, just when I'm hooked
on the children, relearning my grandmother role.

Straight-backed, she goes through the airport
checkpoint, dwindling but undiminished
with the baby in her sling, the other two up ahead

in transit already. Her thoughts will be homing.
She is the home place of my thoughts.
Let there be no corridor down which she disappears.

In blue delight

That nanosecond of waking time
before you turn into
the nightmare from pregnancy

born talking, knowing everything . . .
At the edge of my dream
Pablo runs into the sea and out again.

Cloud Mountain's back
beneath a moon like one of the Dragon Lady's
fingernail clippings.

In dawn that has no Belfast parallel
the gentle rocks that guard this inlet
take on definition.

Exactitude doesn't matter;
what matters is pattern, profusion,
variations on a theme.

The way the clouds in their morning progress
are all skewed east
in the shape of the wind

and how the sand in an envy of ripples
emulates the dip swirl, under over,
forward and back of last night's high tide.

I could go on – about
the seaweed's branching argument
against a life of single purpose;

the jellyfish, starfish, shellfish
arrayed in elaborate codes – but
the sun is shining, and the sky,

having exhausted shades of blue
from indigo to skimmed milk,
reverberates cerulean.

Beach picnic with Aunts

Stepping like cranes
Beth and Ione, Bertha and Louise
– all the aunts on my mother's side –
arrange a picnic on this beach
in a country they've never visited.

Hope (who has the wayward daughter)
is off searching in rock crannies
for wild flowers to domesticate
and before she gets back
there's something I want to say to them

about sisterhood and solidarity,
but they've unfolded the tablecloth
and they're setting out
Jello salad with cottage cheese
Jello salad with grated carrots

Jello salad with pineapple
potato salad, potato chips
fried chicken, sliced ham
devilled eggs, devil's food cake
and a bottle of unfermented grape juice.

Gobsmacked at this spread of love
I'm back in the kitchen at a family reunion
lost in a forest of giant aunts
one of whom reaches down, pats my head
and points me towards my mother.

Between me and all harm

for Ann McGonagle

Carefully – like the girl with buckle boots
who fitted her feet to the holes
her brother punched in crusted snow –

I step into autumn wilderness
letting my wellingtons feel the way
uphill, off solid ground.

Through springy rain-drenched
heather, colonies of flamboyant grasses,
the turning tongues of ferns

there is time
for the art nouveau swank
of a cluster of harebells

rocks appliquéd in orange lichen,
seed pods of rushes
incised with hieroglyphs

the brush strokes
of a stand of reeds, advertising
a new school of calligraphy.

Below me, small boats
and their doubles, at anchor
in the crook of Tulaigh Oileán

a soundless tide moving up
the front beach and the Boggy Strand,
cutting off the bight

flooding the path that Susie took
herding cows to Rinn Raithní
and herding them home again.

On top of the known world
a slow whirl
brings half the county to view.

Errigal, Cruit and Aranmore,
and on the horizon looking south
the far promise of Slieve League

older and less spectacular
than the peaks
that ringed my childhood.

Stranger at the beach

Out he strides across the sand
to the rocks, where he shucks his clothes
and goes into the water.

I follow him from the window
while the clouds turn
gold, pink, purple-grey

reliving the shock of the cold,
floating like branched seaweed
torn from its holdfast

remembering the naked night
when four of us
swam in the North Sea

outlined in living light,
and every move we made
sparked neon choreography.

Not that body, not this beach.
Young and unaware, he comes out of the water,
dresses, walks away.

In the lavender room
for Barbara

Diffused through a bottle of eau naturelle
the rising sun projects a green transparency
over the white duvet on the lavender bed.

Filling my sleep like a travelogue
your panoramic Hawaiian beach
on the whitewashed wall behind my head.

At the Rotonde in Sigean, while we
drank coffee and wine and rum
next to the parrot who never said a word

strangers within our layered selves
wrapped against the tramontane
spoke to each other, and were heard.

Traveller's tale

When the scree starts to slide and you realise
the path you're on above the Med
is a track made by animals, none of them human

you're stuck fast in a blackberry thicket
on the first day of the hunting season
with the baying of hounds getting nearer

knee-deep in a freezing bog
on the shadowy side of a mountain
in the least-inhabited county in Ireland

refer to memory:

over the hill you scrabble up
clutching at roots, on hands and knees,
Auden's ploughman is working his field

the dogs veer off after wild boar
the hunters give you *Bonjour, Madame*
the brambles reluctantly let you go

helped by a man who's herding cows
you pull yourself onto solid ground
and follow the bootprints of others home.

Second nature
for Betty Solomon

Getting into bed, I wear
the blue Sea Island nightshirt
you sent to ease Belfast barbarity.

I like you
wrapped around me –
one fat woman inside
another.

Since you so inconsiderately
died and went to catlovers' heaven
I've put a phone upstairs
so I can get bad news
in the middle of the night
when it always happens

and yesterday
I followed a Michelin woman in a down jacket
down the street for blocks
for her straight white flyaway hair
her flatfooted shortsighted plonk-'em-down-anywhere walk,
expecting a miracle.

When we first met, on a campus
corroded by religion and cold war,
you introduced complexity like a solvent –
the older woman with an interesting past
and several futures.

Knowing wrong from right
I chose guilt by association, renouncing
the god who would never have let you
into our heaven.

Oldest, most unpredictable and constant friend.
On bad days, only your outraged bellow.

On good days, you're huffing along beside me
refusing to let emphysema stop you exploring
Arlands Strand at low tide.

Inlets of poetry, the twisting tracks of love.

Sally on the phone
for Sally Abeles

Your instrumental voice
spanning octaves and oceans
said not to worry
said you were a medical wonder,
crushed, carved, but mending
and still given to logorrhoea.
I couldn't get a word in edgeways.

The drifting boys and girls
who found a haven
in the loft below the Square;
old friends, for whom your voice
was a beacon, pulsing life;
if you spoke now
we'd wait forever to interrupt.

Haikai for an October beach

Visiting this beach
does more than eye doctors can
to cure bad vision

deep in a rock cleft
the white gleam of fallen stars
waiting for water

cat's-eyes in late sun
deliquescing jellyfish
warn my naked feet

every step I take
across the low-tide seafloor
sets off a fresh quake

spouting their alarm
freaked-out razorfish clam up
and dive for cover

when it's time to go
I sweep the sand off my feet
back from where it came

leaving the chalet
as I found it: a clean shell
for passing hermits

the Dungloe bus comes
down from a night sky half storm
half glittering stars.

Will you miss me when I'm gone

The night before they headed home
my granddaughters danced in the living room
around their mother, the furniture and me
to the songs on a bluegrass CD.

They danced high, wide and handsome,
acrobatics, ballet, square dance steps
they learned from TV,
putting their own harmony

to plangent, luxuriant laments
like the ones I got from the radio
and sang to myself, growing up,
rehearsing for a life misspent.

And for the length of the song
they liked the best
            (we played it twice)
I could have died and gone to heaven.

Stocktaking

Check body parts   no

first, access the file
where you dump old news
that doesn't bear thinking about.

Some of them were the enemy

some were their own worst enemies

(and stood up, spoke out
when everybody knew the thing to do
was get on with your life   keep your head down
pray)

most of them were uninvolved
but stood out anyway, accidents of
birth   place   work   faith   loving

the children were wholly innocent

none of them asked for it.

The limestone pavement of the garrigue
                    that has soaked up sun all day
glows bone white in the moonlight

the air's so thick it's difficult
    to breathe.

Close the file   they remain   unaccounted
and it doesn't bear thinking about.

En vacances
for Juli

You know the place I mean,
the one we bussed or hitched or took the train to
summer after summer.

But when I wake
full of plans to return to those jigsaw cliffs,
the headland where you could overdose
on the smell of coconut ice-cream

that crescent beach encroached upon
by sprawling sunstruck dunes

the name's away, the land turned fey
and no map corresponds to the route
that winds through my night-time brain.

And maybe it wasn't you I went with,
or maybe that's where you've gone.

After the Invasion of Iraq

When Juli's platoon was liberating France
in nineteen forty-four, some green GIs –
whose only experience of countryside
was six weeks' basic in the Georgia swamps –
mistook the prickly smell of drying hay
for poison gas, and panicked for their masks.

Images of maimed and dying children
embedded in my head, I circle
the ruined Victorian fountain in Dunville Park.
Essence of cut grass bleeds into the air.

After the protests, the fait accompli.
If he'd been here to see our latest war
presented as a fireworks display,
his anger would have found me better words.

What did you do in the war?

The last summer of the war
the man I was going to marry
was shipped home from Germany
to a transit camp in California
where he got weekend passes to LA
to hear a new kind of jazz called bebop
played by a cat named Dizzy Gillespie
while he waited to invade Japan
and me and my best friend Gay
sewed print cotton shirts on a treadle Singer
to wear outside our blue jeans.

When it began we ran around the playground
shouting *War!* but with no brothers
old enough to die it didn't much signify
although we drew pictures of our planes
shooting lines of dashes at their planes
collected floss that got up your nose
from the milkweeds that grew along the ditchbank
saved the tinfoil from sticks of chewing gum
picked spuds alongside German POWs
guarded by East Coast GIs who did all our lifting
and spent Home Economics crocheting lace
onto washcloths we sent to unknown soldiers
with candy bars and letters of love.

His war was 18-year-olds against 16-year-olds
in the freezing Belgian mud.
Triple rations for Thanksgiving Dinner.
Moving fast after the Bulge
with no time to take prisoners.
Busted from corporal back to PFC
for fraternising with the enemy
by giving a German boy a candy bar.
Even in our worst arguments
when I'd throw his favourite plates
across the kitchen, aimed to miss,
he never resorted to violence.
I think he'd had enough of fighting.

Open Season

September in France is cooler and cheaper
but it's also the start of the hunting season
and I hate the sound of the hounds.

On days when hunting's allowed
the jeeps and vans and four-wheel drives
go past before sun-up

returning late in the afternoon
full of exhausted dogs and hunters
with the kill hidden in a metal box.

There are no bodies lashed
across the hood, like the corpse
of the one deer my father shot.

His timing was bad; we'd just seen Bambi.
And my mother couldn't disguise the taste
of the venison we had to eat for weeks.

Here, wild boar is the main game
and having tasted it once
I don't believe they shoot for the pot.

Lily went for the hunter
who stopped his jeep outside the bergerie
one morning. By a combination

of mime and basic French
shouted over her growls
while I held her lead with both hands

he made me understand his dog
had been lost three days in the scrub,
and if it came to the house

I should ring him at the number
on its collar. No need to be
afraid, the dog was muzzled.

Feeding Lily, I listened
for the sound of a dog that couldn't
kill or eat, or lap up water.

Two days later, when we were
out walking in a harvested vineyard
so Lily could glean her favourite treat –

a red bandanna round her neck
to distinguish her from a wild boar –
he drove up beside us

and gestured to the scrub behind him,
where seven or eight buzzards circled low.
Now I hate the hunters, not the hounds.

At the Gold Rush Museum

Next to the cloisonné Chinese embroidery scissors
in the good-luck shape of a crane

below the king-sized patchwork quilt
pieced by the wife of a prominent businessman
and backed with the tops of men's old socks

I'd put the denim and corduroy dresses
stitched by hand for my daughter
when I was lost in a new country.

Made as pastime, not from need,
they do and don't belong,
like the flower-encrusted pillowcases
stored in my cedarwood hope chest
against the day that I would marry
in the Temple of the Lord in the Land of Zion.

Was it a lifetime's diversion
for the wife of the prominent businessman
waiting for him to wear holes in all of those toes?

No information is given
about the woman who used the scissors.

I imagine her in the Beautiful Country,
new to that raw Gold Mountain town,
working red, gold and emerald threads
onto a pair of black silk slippers.

Country music
for Eilish Martin

My first time alone in the city
I bought a porcelain china shepherdess
with two implausible white-faced lambs
folded beneath her brittle petticoats.

Boxed
and tied in ribbons curled on the store clerk's scissors
she was a present for my mother, although
it wasn't Christmas, it wasn't her birthday
and I wasn't a giving daughter.

The box I kept my mother in was labelled
'finished with babies'. Doing the Sunday dishes
to bluegrass on the radio, I'd found baby bottles
hidden behind the last of her wedding china
in the cupboard where she kept things from the children.

Her forced apology – for what must have been
an open secret – shames me to this day.

Handed across the gap between us,
the shepherdess stood untouched, except for dusting,
on the chiffonier in my parents' bedroom
while I fretted the summer away, addled
by too much country music,
vowing I would never be a wife.

My serene and tangible mother
got on with her flesh-and-blood life.

The icing on the cake

Alchemy and two spoonfuls of liquid
transformed a mountain of powdered sugar

into a pearly translucent glop
you had to spread fast before it set.

Finessing the final, even glaze
with a knife dipped in warm water

never really worked for me,
I was left with ridges and hollows;

obliterate one ridge, get another.
Secretly the patterns pleased me –

drifted snow after a blizzard,
crisscross crests of Saharan sand –

and I didn't want the job to end.
Which might explain why, on windless days

when the sea is shaped by fading
memories of mid-Atlantic storms

I can spend hours becalmed on this beach
tranced by the surge and retreat of the waves

that spread intersecting ridges and hollows
over and over the level sand.

Winding down

The road cuts back upon itself
like the edge of a frond of dulse

until the clouds I turned my back on
confront me, trailing tentacles of rain.

Posters for a Hallowe'en rave
no brighter than the orange bracken.

Walking beside a beach cobbled with
sand-dusted jellyfish after the storm

I'm breathing the freshest air in Europe.
Overhead, a lonesomeness of curlews.

Short of breath in the middle of the night
I wake to the wheeze of high tide

equally afraid of ever / never
lighting another cigarette.

When I am dead – bravado helps me
say it – the sea will do my breathing.

Dancing with my Dad

He didn't look like a dancer.
I'd look away when he made a beeline
for me among the wallflowers

but he waltzed with precision and delicacy
and thanks to him, I was half-
prepared for the ceilidh on Tory

where the men of the place
grabbed the women
and spun us around the hall.

Bottled next morning
into my sleeping bag,
scared to roll over

in case I rolled off
the island that stood to the plane of the sea
like a mesa over the desert

I thought of my father
and how he would have enjoyed that dance;
how I never acknowledged his grace.

The power you gain by outliving.
Hostage in the hands of memory,
the farmer I knew –

who stood out from his neighbours
because he talked with his hands,
and wouldn't put up the price of hay

when hay was scarce in a hard winter,
or keep the government grants for not planting
crops he hadn't planned to –

can no more refuse the dance
than I could then.
We turn this way and that

while I tell him
he's one of the reasons
I married a black-haired man.

On the Friday

Yesterday
the surprise of a steam train
crossing the Lagan twice
and vanishing behind Tomb Street GPO
before my brain could accept
an image belonging to childhood and old movies,
a rhythm nearly as inward
as the beat of my heart.

Watching its smoke pollute the atmosphere magnificently,
wondering how far the molecules
would travel on the wind.

Wondering whether,
if molecules were tagged like migrating birds,
you could know whose last breath
you were breathing?

Today, on my birthday,
I'm here again

trying to make sense
of having been born, grown up, grown old
in a world
               where news of the slaughter of children
is easier to credit than a steam engine out of its time.

Seventy-one years lucky,
and my parents were lucky too.

Beach clean

Incoming tide and offshore wind
are fighting over a large dark flexible object
that's beyond me
       too far out to interpret
              and shouldn't be in the sea.
A pretzel, a hoop, a Moebius strip   or,
Houdini, chained in a black sack.

Keeping one eye on its landward progress
       (in case it's a new form of flotsam)
I keep on collecting the mostly plastic rubbish
exposed by the storms that flattened the bent grass,
into a sculptural heap I'll disguise with bladderwrack
so nobody mistakes it for the local tip.

Plastic hit this beach late.
         Fifty years ago
a man harvesting seaweed at Arlands found a ping pong ball
and kept it, as the egg of an unknown bird, until
another man, back from the States, enlightened him
       – and then there was the mystery of how it got among the kelp.

Growing up, I hated
the no-colour Tupperware, primary-coloured plates and bowls
that felt greasy even after you washed them
            and had no weight and no backstory.
Interest was supplied
by a misread article in the *Reader's Digest:*

plastics retained molecular memory
and might, under certain conditions,
revert (like people) to their original form.
Heat was such a condition.
However hot the dishwater, it never happened.

Held in a memory that cannot dim
no matter how fragmented
this plastic rubbish
terribly remains
its self.

I pick no-colour   primary-colour   kindergarten shapes
out of the bent   the water   the sand
wade in and retrieve the large dark object
– a plastic bin with its bottom stove in.

Take the discarded container
for the discarded things contained
and make it my centrepiece.